Will Our Tears Forever Flow

A Father's Story of Grief and Hope

Ted L. Wampler

Copyright © 2000

Published by:
> Tennessee Valley Publishing
> PO Box 52527
> Knoxville, Tennessee 37950-2527

Printed and bound in the United States of America.

Second printing

Library of Congress Catalog Card No. 00-109226

ISBN 1-882194-72-1

Dedicated
to the Memory of
Mary Lee Wampler Hitch

Beloved daughter, sister, wife, mother, school teacher, church leader, and friend—Mary Lee was many things to many people. Above all else she was a true Christian, showing countless acts of kindness to others. May the light of her life never go out.

(Bulletin, White Wing Church of the Nazarene, Pastor Richard Hutchison)

ACKNOWLEDGMENTS

We, the parents of Mary Lee, thank Dr. Richard Dew, chapter leader, and our other Compassionate Friends who were there for us helping with our grief during our early months.

Thanks to our immediate family, extended family, neighbors, friends, and business associates who helped us to bear our grief.

We want to thank pastor Richard Hutchison and our church family at White Wing Church of the Nazarene for their prayers and extended support.

I also want to thank our Compassionate Friends for the knowledge we gained from them that was helpful in writing this book. I especially thank all the unknown sources—the books and articles I have read, the speakers I've heard— who have contributed to this book ideas whose origin I no longer remember.

A special thanks to our friend Connie Jordan Green who put the material in order and edited this book.

I

The phone rang at 8:30 p.m. I immediately recognized my son-in-law Al Hitch's voice when I picked up the receiver. "Have you heard anything about Mary Lee being in a wreck?" he asked.

Al had been away from home that evening and had received a call that there had been an automobile accident and the police were at his home waiting to talk to him. He called us from his cellular phone as he headed home. Our daughter Mary Lee, his wife, who already had a master's degree, was commuting to Tennessee Technological University for another degree.

Until Al's phone call, Thursday, October 5, 1995, had been a day of routine work for me. It had stormed the night before and continued to rain much of the day. The sun came out in midafternoon, but we still had gusts of wind. A touch of fall was in the East Tennessee air, maples beginning to turn orange, yellow, and red, joining the glowing reds of dogwood and sassafras.

After I left my office, I picked up limbs from our yard and also, with my cousin Brenda's help, at my mother's home nearby. As we worked, I noticed unusually heavy traffic, including many big trailer trucks, on Highway 70 that runs in front of our homes. I knew either a bad wreck or some type construction had shut down Interstate 40.

My wife, Frances, and I had a big weekend planned. We were to host a reunion picnic for my high school graduating class. Invitations had been sent, and people were coming from different sections of the country. When I came home,

Frances had gone to dinner with a group of her high school classmates. Sometime shortly after 6 p.m. I retired to my study to prepare a Sunday School lesson to teach the following Sunday. It was a very quiet time for me with no one in the house. The only out of the ordinary sound was from the heavy flow of traffic on Highway 70 beyond my window.

In making my notes for the Sunday School class, I wrote, "If you have never had a storm in your life, the storm clouds could be gathering now." I do not remember the title of that lesson nor the scripture that went with it. Looking back now, five years later, I wish I had not destroyed the notes. The only part of my notes I remember is the above quote. Little did I realize those words were actually for me. I was now living in the last hours of the life I had known. Within a short period of time my life and the lives of all my family were to be forever changed.

Frances came home around 8:30 from her dinner. Soon after her arrival, the call came from Al. Frances and I are fortunate to have all four of our children and their families living nearby. Three of them work in our family business, and all, including spouses and grandchildren, phone or stop by frequently. However, the phone was eerily quiet after Al's call. Frances and I felt we needed to get over to Al and Mary Lee's house to be with the children. She went into the kitchen to put some food back into the refrigerator, and I went into the bedroom to change my shoes. We both were hurrying, knowing that something was seriously wrong. Al had told us someone had been airlifted by Life Star helicopter from the accident scene.

A little later, around 9:00 John Edd, our youngest son, stepped in the door of our sun porch. Frances came out of the kitchen, and I came from the master bedroom into the sun porch. John Edd, with his voice breaking, said, "I love both of you, we all do, and I hate to tell you."

I said, "Mary Lee has been killed."

At the same time, Frances said, "She's dead."

"Yes," John Edd said.

Frances slumped into a chair. The accident had occurred at 5:50 on Interstate 40 near our home. The heavy traffic past our house had been the result of vehicles being detoured around the accident scene.

The storm clouds had moved into our lives, and that night we began a long journey of grief, one for which nothing in our earlier life had prepared us.

ℬ

I had grown up as a happy child in rural East Tennessee. Most of my preteen years were spent on a farm during the Great Depression of the 1930s. My family knew what poverty and physical labor were all about. My dad and mother both worked long hard hours. I was also taught to do my part at a very early age. I still feel that as long as there's work to do and I feel like doing it, that is living life at its best.

One of my favorite pastimes was running the hills and woods with my dog, looking for whatever a boy and his dog might find. Many years have now come and gone; oftentimes my mind wanders back to those same hills and woods with my dog, Rounder. I also enjoyed fishing in the creek, along with playing in the water. It was fun to catch June bugs, tie them by the hind leg, and, while holding onto the other end of the string, watch them fly. Lightning bugs were also plentiful in the summer, and I, like most children, enjoyed catching them, putting them in jars, and watching them light up the jar. I also looked forward to going barefoot in the summer. Shoes were only for church and school.

When I got home from school, I had many chores to do. I had to feed the chickens, gather eggs, feed and milk the cow, carry in plenty of wood and water, and close the hen house door just before dark in order to keep foxes and other animals out. In the fall, I gathered lots of walnuts for my mother to make pies and other goodies.

I tried to get a little spending money and some to save if I could from trapping muskrats and selling their skins, catching minnows and selling them for fish bait, and for sure picking and selling blackberries.

When I was eleven years old, a little nine-year-old girl named Frances Wilburn moved with her family from Indiana to Tennessee. She got my attention immediately and has had it ever since. There is a phrase I like to use: "The great big doors of history swing on little hinges." Needless to say, from the time Frances arrived in the community, I wanted to be a regular at church every Sunday to see her. Her presence also gave me reason for going to school when school was in session. Ten years after we met, in December 1950, I came home from the Army on furlough and she became my wife. We had some break-ups a few times before we were married, but the make-ups made the break-ups worthwhile. Frances soon joined me at Fort Devens, Massachusetts, and we started on what has now been a long journey together.

4

In December 1951, our first daughter, Ruth Ann, was born at Fort Devens; believe me, we were happy parents. In early 1952, the Army came up with a point system that allowed me to get an early discharge even before the Korean War was over. In May 1952 I brought my family back home to Tennessee, and Frances joined me in building a successful business, at the time called Wampler's Wholesale Meats, a business that had been reopened in 1947 before I was called into the service in 1950.

I have always believed that success cannot be measured by where we get to in life but by where we come from. By way of illustration, here is a little history about that business success.

My parents, Edith and Riley M. Wampler, began the business as a small operation, making sausage in their farmhouse kitchen, located in the Eaton Crossroads community of Lenoir City, Tennessee. In 1937 Dad built a small tin shack, for hog kill only, on the creek near his farm home. The total cost of materials for the building was $38. A short while later he built a much nicer building for both cattle and hog slaughter. Hogs were killed in the winter only, but cattle were killed year-round and the meat was delivered hot to markets in town that had coolers. The operation, known as Wampler's Slaughter House, closed some time during World War II.

The business reopened when I graduated from high school in 1947. Dad and I, with money hard to come by, each invested $1100. My money came mostly from childhood savings earned by picking and selling blackberries and selling fish bait. We bought our first cooler, a small six-by-eight, and changed the business name to Wampler's Wholesale

Meats. My cousin, Harry W. Wampler, soon joined us. In 1953 the company became a corporation, and in 1981 the name was changed to Wampler's Farm Sausage Company.

The company is now one of the most modern, sanitary meat plants in the industry. Wampler's retail sausage is enjoyed and served proudly in homes throughout the Southeast under the Wampler's name as well as under many private label brands. Our institutional sausage distribution has grown to include most of the United States.

While our business was growing, our family also grew. Mary Lee was born in 1955, Ted Jr. in 1958, and John Edd in 1960. All four of our children were, and still are, special to us. We had lots of fun in our home, and I hope their memories of home are pleasant. A bumper sticker I saw recently gave me another reason to be glad for our good times. The sticker read: "Be good to your children; they decide which nursing home to put you in."

Along with the playful hours we had together, we also all worked hard in the sausage business. John Edd, in a talk to a group, said that anytime he and his brother were out of school his daddy expected them to work at least a half-day, and he did not really care which twelve hours it was.

During the children's teenage years, Frances would never go to sleep until all the children were in. I believe the first question she will ask when she reaches her eternal destiny with Mary Lee will be, "Are all the children and grandchildren in?" If the answer is no, she will be waiting just inside the eastern gate.

The following anonymous poem is dedicated to Frances.

ARE ALL THE CHILDREN IN?

I think of the times as the night
draws nigh of an old house on the hill,
of a yard all wide and blossom-starred
where the children played at will.
And when the night at last came down,
hushing the merry din,
Mother would look around and ask,
"Are all the children in?"
'Tis many and many a year since then,
and the old house on the hill
no longer echoes to childish feet,
and the yard is still, so still.
But I see it all, as the shadows creep,
and though many years have been
since then, I can hear Mother ask,
"Are all the children in?"
I wonder if when the shadows fall
on the last short, earthly day,
when we say goodby to the world outside,
all tired with our childish play,
when we step out into that other land
where mother so long has been,
will we hear her ask, just as of old,
"Are all the children in?"

After we become a parent we remain a parent as long as we live, and our children remain our children as long as we live. As our children became adults they also became our best friends. All are highly honorable and are respected in the community. Our relationship with them became deeper as we shared our joys and our sorrows. Mary Cleckley, in an article in *We Need Not Walk Alone* (published by Compassionate Friends, 1990), points out that, as our children age, our concern changes from worrying about what would happen to them if something happened to us to a worry about what would happen to us if something happened to them. They become our security blanket.

Three of our four children joined the family business right after they finished college. The business has had tremendous growth with their added leadership. Mary Lee chose to be a school teacher.

As I said earlier, our children and their families all live close to us. We see them or talk to them by phone almost every day. Our home is an after-church gathering place for food and fellowship for all the family. Until the time of Mary Lee's death our family consisted of our four children, their spouses, our ten grandchildren, and our foster daughter Karen. We had the ideal American family, and then tragedy struck a devastating blow.

We have a tendency to believe if we work hard, pay our bills, be good to our family, treat our fellow man right, and go to church, we have some kind of protection. We tend to forget that we are human and subject to the tragedies that are common to man. The truth is we are all just one phone call or knock on the door away from having our lives changed forever.

The sudden news of Mary Lee's death hit like a blow to my entire body. For at least a year I felt physically as if I had been knocked down by a trailer truck. I became obsessed with a mental image of Mary Lee that lasted for weeks. It caused me to fear I might be losing my mind.

The shock that comes with such news is a blessing in a way; in such a state we cannot fully take in what we have been told. We go into denial, feeling that the bad news is a mistake. We move back and forth from shock into intense grief, our bodies operating on their own timetable.

Acceptance of the death of one of our children is very difficult. Different people require various periods of time before reality sets in. My own grief seemed to worsen seven to nine months after Mary Lee's death. I finally had to accept the fact that she is gone, she is not coming back, and I will never see her again in this life.

Grief has been mankind's universal language since the beginning of humanity. Our first parents, Adam and Eve, knew the heartache of standing over the dead body of their murdered son. One of my cousins, Newell Grimes, who is a registered nurse, told me many years ago that when a baby was born at the hospital, one of her first thoughts was that someday someone would have to grieve the death of that person. I always expected to grieve for my parents, grandparents, uncles, aunts, perhaps some cousins, but surely not for my children.

The death of a child probably causes the most severe grief any human will ever face, a grief that creates almost unbearable pain. Grief is the price we pay for love—the greater the love, the greater the grief. Whatever blesses our hearts can also break our hearts. We will all be separated at some time from everything in this world we hold dear. It will either leave us or we will leave it.

Frances and I, realizing early on that no two people grieve the same, gave each other permission to each grieve his or her own way. We have remained very understanding of one another. Our emotional makeup is different and we respect that difference.

Daytime has been more difficult for me and night for Frances. During the first year after Mary Lee's death I cried uncontrollably during a large part of my day; for Frances crying was almost nonstop during the night. I thought many times of a Bible verse Dr. Richard Dew, who is also a member of The Compassionate Friends, uses as an epigraph for his book, *Rachel's Cry*: "Rachel, weeping for her children, refusing to be comforted, because they are no more" (Jeremiah 31:15).

Frances and I visited Mary Lee's grave at various hours of the day and night, sometimes together, sometimes alone. We often just felt the need to be near her body. For me, being alone at the grave in the darkness of night provided an opportunity to cry until I could cry no more. I felt better afterwards. Cold winter nights seem to be hard for both of us, especially if the ground is covered with a blanket of snow. Parental instinct causes us to want to bring the body in where it is warm.

The first year after Mary Lee's death was for me just one long endless day. Frances and I both began to lose our desire to live, a situation that broke our hearts as we looked at our other children, whom we love the same as we love Mary Lee, and at our grandchildren. We didn't want our other children to think we were putting the deceased child on a pedestal above them.

Grief is hard work. It's accompanied by deep and lasting questions about our lives, about what we are experiencing. We ask: Why are we tired all the time? Why is it almost impossible to concentrate or to become interested in anything? What is going to happen to us?

The death of a child puts a particular strain on a marriage. Divorce is not uncommon in the years immediately following the death. Now, after many years together, as Frances and I look at one another, we share our common grief.

WILL OUR TEARS FOREVER FLOW

II

Our entire community did everything they could to try to help us after Mary Lee's death; our family will never forget the outpouring of support. On the day of her funeral, her home church, Dixie Lee Baptist, broke ground for a new building which has been named "The Mary Lee Hitch Family Life Center." Her husband, Al Hitch, was minister of music there at the time of her death. Mary Lee loved her church, and they loved her and her family.

Eaton Elementary School, where she taught first grade for nineteen years, established a scholarship in her memory. Many books were donated to the library because of her love for reading. The Parent Teacher Organization prepared a beautiful reading memorial garden at the school. We will always remember the love and respect she had for Larry Duff, Eaton principal, and for all the faculty, staff, and her students.

Even our doberman dog seemed to try in his own way to share our sorrow. For several nights after Mary Lee's death, the dog howled, something he had never done before and has not done since. His howl was a mournful, wailing cry. My good friend Dr. Ager Vanderburg, a retired Methodist minister, told me he believes a dog can sense when his or her master is in sorrow, and I agree.

I longed to find something that would "fix me." I wanted to read every book about grief that I could get my hands on. In bookstores I searched out books that never before had caught my attention. I lost a considerable amount of weight and knew I was going to have to have some help from someone somewhere. Frances and I could not provide much support for each other as we each had all we could handle on our own.

About this time our daughter, Ruth Ann, heard of a support group called "The Compassionate Friends." She felt her mother and I should go for help. At 2 p.m. on the second Sunday in November, we attended our first meeting at Second United Methodist Church, Knoxville, Tennessee. As we pulled into the church parking lot, Frances said, "I don't think I can do this. I don't believe I can stand it."

I said, "I know I'm going in. I must have help."

We got out of the car and walked slowly in together. We were met with love and understanding. Some people there were far along in their grief. Some of them were helping themselves to refreshments while talking and laughing. The laughing at first was a turn-off for me, but it later became my hope that I too could someday laugh again.

The meeting started with some discussion about having a Christmas gathering. I had no interest whatsoever in any kind of social function. I wanted help and I wanted it now. Then the time came for each of us to introduce ourselves and our spouse, along with the name, age, and cause of our child's death. I don't think I made it all the way through my introduction. Others were there also who were not very far along in their grief, and their introductions too were a struggle. Fortunately, there is never any pressure on anyone to talk. If you feel that you can't talk, you are just to nudge the person next to you.

By the time each person had told when and how his or her child died, tears flowed freely. Next came two hours of sharing. Frances and I both felt totally exhausted when the meeting was over. I have never been as tired in my life. I felt that we had now taken on all of the others' sorrows on top of our own, and I didn't know if we could ever go back. However, as the time for the next month's meeting approached, we wanted to go back. After about three meetings, we realized we were being helped by the group. The meetings soon became the only thing we really wanted to go to.

We had lots of invitations out to eat and invitations to people's homes, but we declined all invitations until sometime in January. We did accept an invitation to the home of Janie Amburn, a member of our church family. Janie has had a lot of tragedy in her life, including the death of two husbands and her daughter. Her daughter Vicki was a highly esteemed I.C.U. nurse, an outstanding person whom everyone loved. I knew if anyone could understand, Janie could. It would be okay to cry at her house and not feel bad about it. Janie is an inspiration in that her faith has remained strong. We don't share our grief with each other much any more; however, she still has that look in her eyes of the person who has lost a child.

There are many things to deal with and to try to work through after the death of one's child. According to the accident report, Mary Lee was traveling west on Interstate 40 and left the roadway to the left, going onto the grass median. She attempted to re-enter the west-bound lanes, but oversteered to the left, going across the grass median onto the east-bound lanes of Interstate 40. She was struck by a car and a tractor-trailer traveling east on Interstate 40.

Most parents try to find something or someone to blame. Some, when they can't find any specific thing to blame, even blame God. In our case, we had many questions that we wondered about: Did the bright sun in the west temporarily blind Mary Lee? Was she attempting to use a cell phone? Was she putting a cassette in a tape player? Was she in someone's blind spot, who cut over too quickly in front of her? Was she a victim of road rage for driving slower in the passing lane than someone thought she should? Did that person pass her on the right and deliberately cut back too quickly in front of her? Did the vehicle malfunction in some way? Did she have a tumor or some physical problem?

We will never know the answer to the above questions. In addition to wondering about the cause of the accident, we were tortured by thoughts of her last moments. Was she screaming? Was she crying? Was she even conscious? Did she think of Al and the children? Was she praying? How horrible were her last few moments of life? Why should anyone have to die such a violent death?

All these and similar things must be worked through in the grief process. We can run these things and others through our minds over and over, but no matter what the answer to any of our questions is, nothing can change what happened nor bring her back. The what-ifs must also be dealt with, even though they can't change anything either.

As the months went by our Compassionate Friends family came to mean more and more to us. It also became clear to us that it was necessary for some people at the meetings to be far along in their grief. If all in attendance were newly bereaved parents, no one would be able to help the others.

Parents of all ages may find themselves in need of emotional support and come to realize they have a long journey ahead of them. We also find ourselves in need of physical support. Meeting with the Compassionate Friends helps to meet both kinds of needs, the physical presence of others who have grieved through the loss of a child and yet are able to function in society giving encouragement as we struggle through each day. The doors of the Compassionate Friends are open to anyone, families and individuals, who have lost a child. I have heard it said, "There are no dues or fees of any kind to pay, yet we are the organization with the highest dues in the world." The cost is the life of a child.

Despite its value to us, the Compassionate Friends may not meet all the needs of everyone. Some bereaved parents have problems that are spiritual, and they need to talk to their pastor, priest, rabbi, or other spiritual leaders. The Compassionate Friends has no affiliation with any religion. Some parents may need to see a professional counselor. Some may need to see a physician for medication. The Compassionate Friends does not try to infringe on the areas of expertise of professionals.

Actually, quite a few of our calls on the contact line are referrals from the above. The Compassionate Friends has a contact voicemail number listed in the Yellow Pages under support groups. I return most of those calls to people throughout central East Tennessee. None of us knows how the other person feels, but people have a real need to talk with someone who understands their grief. Frances and I have become very active in the Knoxville Hope Chapter of the Compassionate Friends. She is at present the outreach person. As such, she checks the obituary list every day and contacts the funeral homes for addresses of parents to whom she sends information about the Compassionate Friends.

Our qualifications for a ministry of mercy came to us without our choosing. Certainly, given a choice, we would elect to have Mary Lee back and forgo the bitterly earned qualifications that enable us to help others. But our only choice was to use or not use the knowledge we have obtained. I believe the gift of mercy is a gift from God. In a letter to the Romans, Paul reminds that "those who offer comfort to the sorrowing should do so with Christian cheer" (12:8, *The Living Bible*). It is our desire for the Lord to use us in the ministry of reaching out with compassion to parents with aching hearts. A lot of hurt in this world is hidden behind smiles, to be replaced with crying when the person is alone. Many people need someone who really cares and understands. We listen with our hearts and respond from our hearts. In the Compassionate Friends group we hear each other talk, and we learn from each other. The more we learn, the more we become qualified to help others.

Frances and I have attended two Compassionate Friends national conferences. We heard excellent speakers and attended grief workshops that were highly educational. All such experiences move us along in our process of healing, and they equip us more fully to minister to others.

Since the death of Mary Lee, I have worn an angel on my shirt collar in her memory. This small pin sparks conversation, often opening doors that would otherwise be inaccessible. For example, recently Frances and I were traveling with her brother Richard Wilburn and his wife Violet, who is my cousin. We stopped in Sikeston, Missouri, at Lamberts' Throw Roll Restaurant. When our waitress commented on my angel, I told her it was in memory of our daughter who was killed. Frances said, "I usually wear one, but have lost mine."

The waitress handed Frances the angel she was wearing. "I want you to have this," she said. Then she told us about the death of her children. We at once were united by a common bond.

III

In addition to coping with our grief over our daughter's death, Frances and I had other sorrows to deal with that first year. We learned, only a few months after Mary Lee's death, that our oldest child, Ruth Ann, and our youngest, John Edd, both had benign tumors near the brain stem. Both required surgery.

Most parents who have lost one child have an intense fear of losing another. Through Compassionate Friends, Frances and I have met people who have lost two, some three, and a few have lost four children. We are more aware than ever that life is uncertain, and death is sure.

Fortunately, Ruth Ann and John Edd's tumors remained dormant for a while and were successfully removed in 1998.

Shortly after we learned about the existence of the tumors, both Frances' mother and my mother died. Not long afterwards, our oldest son, Ted Jr., informed us his marriage was in trouble, news which was also heartbreaking for us. A divorce is a kind of death in itself.

In addition to the other burdens we were struggling under, my cousin Harry Wampler, the person who is nearest to being my brother, had his second open-heart surgery. I stayed at the hospital until the surgery was over and he appeared to be doing well. However, the next day I got a call saying that something had gone wrong. Harry was not expected to live, or if he did survive, he would most likely have suffered brain damage.

For me, that news was "the straw that broke the camel's back." Instead of going straight to the hospital, I lay down in midafternoon, thinking I could not stand much more.

We've all had people tell us God will not put more on us than we can bear up under. Yet we all know people who have crashed or broken down from having more tragedies and burdens than they could endure. The Bible does not tell us that God will not put more on us than we can stand. The Bible does say, "God is faithful, who will not suffer you to be tempted above that ye are able, but will with the temptation also make a way to escape, that ye may be able to bear it" (I Corinthians 10: 13). I think it's significant that the quote includes the word temptation; I feel Paul deals here with the subject of temptation and sin, not the burdens of life.

Again, we were fortunate in that Harry recovered against all odds. Today he lives a life that is normal in every respect except for a few physical limitations.

The only thing I had going for me that first year was teaching a Sunday School class in the Church of the Nazarene. For some reason, I clung to that responsibility. Teaching the class put at least some meaning and purpose into a shattered life. I taught the class many times through bitter tears, but the class members were understanding, and the size of the class continued to grow.

I wish all people realized that the state of being a bereaved parent is not contagious. Being around a parent in grief is not going to cause one's own child to die. More hurt is heaped upon bereaved parents when others shy away from them at a time when friendship and understanding are needed more than ever.

Grief and depression go hand in hand. Dr. Richard Dew reminded me of an old adage: "You can have depression without grief, but you cannot have grief without depression."

Frances and I had a real need to be with people who understood depression and that hopelessness and sadness are not abnormal following the death of a child. We were fortunate in that we found a safe haven in the Compassionate Friends, a place where we can talk about our child and our problems over and over again without fear that someone will say, "We've already discussed that," or "We've heard all that before." Among the participants at a Compassionate Friends meeting, no one will say, "Don't dwell on it"; "You have other children"; "You are not the only one who ever lost a child." Young parents will not be told, "You are young and can still have another child."

I wish all our friends would be unafraid to speak Mary Lee's name. We still love her as much as ever and we always will. As parents we know our children can live on in our hearts as long as we live. They are a part of us, and the love we have in our hearts for them can never be taken away.

Although we will never get over the death of a child, we can get through it. I would like to assure any newly bereaved parents that they will get better. Art Pickle, a trusted friend of many years, told me to be thankful for any improvement I received. He said twenty-five percent of something is better than one hundred percent of nothing. I took that advice seriously and tried from then on to be thankful for any gain I had, instead of concentrating on the mess I was in. I began to look around and tried to count the many blessings I had left, and not focus all my attention on the loss.

I look forward to the day when society will embrace the grieving person and will say, "Tell me about your child. Cry if you wish, pour out your hurts, all your heartache. I will not be judgmental." No message of comfort can be spoken that is greater than the touch of the human hand. A hug or handshake says someone cares. As long as Job's comforters surrounded him with love and concern, they eased his burdens. Only when they began to try to explain his misfortune did they become a part of his burden.

Not only does the death of a child bring numerous changes to the parents' lives, but it also dramatically affects the lives of other members of the family. Many times the siblings are the "forgotten grievers." Mary Lee's death tore the hearts of our other children out by the roots, just as it did the hearts of Frances and me. Neither Ruth Ann, Ted Jr., nor John Edd will ever be the same. By and large, people asked them how their dad and mother were doing; people seldom asked how they were doing. Unfortunately, none of us could be much support to the other. We all had all we could do dealing with our own grief.

Mary Lee is survived by her husband, James Albert Hitch Jr., and two children, Jimmy and Stephanie, who were fifteen and thirteen, respectively, at the time of Mary Lee's death. Shortly after Mary Lee's death, Stephanie wrote a poem which has continued to mean a great deal to all the family.

UNFORGETTABLE

On one unforgettable night it was said
One moment you were there and then you were dead.
The whole world stopped in an unusual way;
You were so full of life, but it was taken away.
There were no obvious reasons, you did nothing wrong
Yet the voice of death called so sudden and strong.
God must have had a reason, this was part of his plan,
For he led you away with his nail-scarred hand.
I remember your sweet smile, the love that you gave,
The times that we shared I will always save.
To know you was to love you, and as everyone knew
No one in need was a stranger to you.
Now I know you're in Heaven and I'll see you someday
But until that time comes I'll just remember and pray.
Sometimes I wish that you were still here
But in my heart I know that you will always be near.

ॐ

Our family is very grateful to Al who did not neglect the children in any way. Through all his grief he tried to be both father and mother. Jimmy graduated from high school as salutatorian and Stephanie as valedictorian. Both are now in college.

23

At the time of Mary Lee's death, a foreign student, Borce Lazarov, was living with her family. He came to live with us in order to finish his schooling in the United States.

Al and his family have remained close to us, and we think of his entire family as an extension of our family. Al has now remarried. His new wife, Cliffreda Gilreath, had been a friend of Mary Lee's from the time they were little girls. We have always known Cliffreda to be a fine person, and we love her. She and Al have built a new home in the subdivision with our other children near our own home.

Nearly three years after the death of Mary Lee, I said to Frances, "We did not have any choice in what happened to us, but we do have a choice in how we use the experience." I was beginning to wonder if we were going to try to put our lives back together or just throw the rest of our lives away. Will Mary Lee be remembered in part by what we do with our lives? I believe most every person has a choice that only he or she can make. Will I become a bitter person, or do I try to become a better person?

Frances and I do not believe God had some reason, plan, or purpose for the death of Mary Lee. We believe that God is "the father of mercies, and the God of all comfort; who comforteth us in all our tribulation" (I Corinthians 1:3-4). We do believe a purpose can be drawn from the experience. We do not want our lives to be in vain. I believe it was Helen Keller who said, "Life is not in vain if you can ease the pain of another."

As time went by, Frances and I became more and more convinced that we should stay with the Compassionate Friends and make ourselves available to help others. Some burdens in life we must bear alone, but other burdens can be shared. Grief is among those that are lightened by sharing. Each time we talk about the death, we heal just a little bit more. We need the support of people who understand and, in some cases, can help give us assurance we aren't going crazy. That sort of support is offered by the Compassionate Friends. Earlier I discussed the first time Frances and I attended a local group meeting. Let me add that it was very difficult for me as a man to step into that group and to admit my life was out of control and needing help. As a general rule, women will more often seek help than will men. We've all heard, and rightly, that men do not like to stop and ask directions if they are lost. Little boys are told when they stump their toe and want to wail that big boys don't cry. Since all little boys want to be big boys, they grow into men trained to choke their emotions. Just as little boys need to cry when they are hurt, so do men. Going to my first Compassionate Friends meeting was a beginning step along a road that led, if not to healing, at least to a place of mending.

A portion of Isaiah 61 speaks directly to Frances and me: "He hath sent me to bind up the broken hearted." We interpret that to mean not just the hearts of those who share our faith, but rather all the broken hearted, those from many different circumstances and religious beliefs.

By allowing God to work through us, becoming His hands on this earth, Frances and I have found a ministry we can do. We have discovered our lives do not have to be in vain. And we have learned the healing value of constructive work.

As bereaved parents, we need to remember that our children would not wish us to continue in intense grief forever. They would want us to laugh again. For a long time after Mary Lee's death, I thought I would never be able to laugh again. If I did happen to laugh, I felt that I had betrayed her in some way or my love for her was less than it had been. In the event I happened to feel the least bit better or have even part of a good day, I felt guilty. We as bereaved parents sometimes make it too hard on ourselves.

Readjustment to and acceptance of life without one's child is never easy. Reaching that stage can be a long journey. I have a picture of Mary Lee on my office desk, along with the serenity prayer. Frances and I also have her picture in the living room of our home with a flickering candle that never goes out.

A national poll showed the majority of people felt grief should be over in six weeks. Most people I know will mourn the death of a pet longer than that. We've all heard that grief can be divided into various stages; I believe those stages can be placed into three headings:

1) Shock;
2) Intense grief;
3) Readjustment.

The information I've learned through the Compassionate Friends, and have gained through experience, is that as a general rule the father will recover to whatever extent he is going to within two to three years, and the mother within three to five years.

In this life our child exists only as memories, memories that we carry and that all who knew her carry. No one can take those memories away from us. We hope others will talk to us about Mary Lee and will not be afraid to call her name or to tell us something about her. If we cry on such occasions, it is not because they have done or said something wrong. Mary Lee's death is the cause of our tears. It would be as difficult not to think about Mary Lee as it would be not to think about our other children. That will never happen. We don't want to be robbed of all we have left of her.

One of the most hurtful things people with good intentions can say is "Get over it." Our grief will never be over. The best illustration I've heard is that of a person who has lost an arm or leg. He or she will never "get over it" but will learn to live with the handicap. A part of that person is gone, and a part of us is gone. Our children are a part of us; we also learn to live with the handicap.

We have also come to the conclusion that life cannot be measured by the time lived, but by the influence or impact the life has upon others. We all, in our walk down the highway of life, come to forks in the road, one of the most important being the point at which we ask, What am I going to do with my life? Mary Lee as a child chose the wise road, one that possesses eternal hope and produces a life that has a meaningful existence, the most rewarding and satisfying life a person can live. We know her life will have an impact on others for many years to come. We're also aware of the long-lasting effect her death has on others, as does the death of any child or young person.

The death of a child probably changes our lives more than any other single event. Frances's and my own intense grief has caused us to be more understanding and compassionate as we reach out to others. If we are stronger in any way at all, it would be that we feel nothing worse is going to happen to us than already has.

We believe that grief is God's medicine for a broken heart. There has to be grief before there can be healing. We know of no easy or simple solutions to grieving. We just have to do the best we can one day at a time. We do thank God for tears that seem to bring some comfort. We also thank God for the healing hand of time that helps all of us to bear our loss, depending upon how we use that time. However, time can work against us as it moves us farther and farther away from the period during which we had our deceased child with us and were able to see her, to hear her voice. Frances and I have found that our faith in God has helped us to work through the grief process, especially as it has provided us with hope of seeing our child again, a hope that allows us to feel with each passing day we draw closer and closer to a reunion with our child. For those without faith in God, the apostle Paul says, "If in this life only we have hope in Christ, we are of all men most miserable" (I Corinthians 15:19). We have found both having faith in God and sharing our grief with others to be helpful in the healing process.

As we look back across the last five years, with all the tears, heartache, and grief, we would choose to experience all that again rather than never to have known Mary Lee at all. God did not take away our grief, but He did give us strength to bear the load and face life honestly. In the midst of the storms of life we still seem to have an inner peace the world cannot give and cannot take away.

Earlier I mentioned the pain Frances and I felt as we stood by Mary Lee's grave in the cold winter months. My visits to the grave seem to be much different in the spring and early days of summer. During those seasons, as I walk through the silent city of the dead, my spirits are lifted by nature's many signs of new life. While I smell the newly mown grass, I see daffodils, day lilies, violets, and peonies bursting with new life. A soft breeze sets the flowers in motion, reminding me of the gently rocking chairs on our porch. Song birds trill their melodies from the grave monuments or from nearby trees. Being surrounded by such abundant life reaffirms my faith in the resurrection of the body. When warmer days of summer come, so do butterflies. Some call them "winged flowers," and rightly so. Looking at a caterpillar, one finds it almost impossible to envision it taking on wings and beauty. If something that looks and acts like a worm can become the winged creatures of beauty that flutter past me, then surely there is hope that our loved ones have taken on a new form of life.

I believe many times God speaks to us through nature. When I vacationed in Florida and watched the sun rise over the ocean, I would think, "Here it comes with full brightness for our part of the world, just as someone on the other side is watching it go out of sight." In the same way, I like to think of our loved ones as just having gone out of our sight, but shining with full brightness on the other side.

Tears are looked at by some people as weakness or lack of faith. Our tears were not because of a lack of faith, but because of the death of our daughter. Faith will not fill the vacant chair nor replace the visits, phone calls, hugs, and a sweet voice saying I love you. At the same time, all religions should bring some comfort. We all need an anchor that will hold before the storms of life move in. None of us can draw on a faith we do not have. On the other hand, some bereaved parents pretend they are getting along better than they are in order to impress their pastor or church family. A man in Nashville told me about a couple in his church who had lost a child. He said God just carried them right through it with no problems. If that were true, then it would be obvious to me that I'm not one of God's favorite children.

Frances and I have never asked God why. The question rather is why not? Why should our children be exempt from tragic accidents and such diseases as brain tumors that are common to mankind? We have never questioned the sunshine in our lives, so why question the storms? I do, however, believe we must ask God the important questions in our lives. If we can't go to God with our questions, where do we turn? Even Jesus Christ said, "My God, my God, why hast Thou forsaken me?" (Matthew 27:46).

Although Frances and I feel we have now reached a stage of normalcy, normal for us will never be the same as it was before Mary Lee's death. Someone has said, "We can't unknow what we know happened." We are not the same people we were, but we are satisfied with the new people we have become. We have tried to find new meaning and purpose in our lives. We have learned to put the problems of life in their proper perspective. Compared to the death of a child most of our problems look small.

I have found being near bodies of water to be comforting. Sitting for hours by a large roaring mountain stream is good medication, as is time spent on the peaceful banks of a nearby lake, where I am reminded of the shepherd David when he said in Psalm 23, "He leadeth me beside the still waters. He restoreth my soul." The last verse of the 23rd Psalm also means a great deal to me because of its message of God's never failing mercy and love: "Surely goodness and mercy shall follow me all the days of my life, and I will dwell in the house of the Lord forever." In the words of the song writer, "The toils of the road will seem nothing when we get to the end of the way."

Will our tears forever flow? Yes. Sometimes just seeing a young couple with two little girls, hearing the girls saying Daddy, Daddy, Daddy, can make me emotional. Certain music, birthdays, holidays, anniversaries, family get-togethers, and many other small events can cause tears to flow. Sometimes our tears flow for no known reason.

Our tears will flow until we draw our last breath and our eyes are closed in death. Only eternity can bring final closure. Heaven to me now means much more than streets of gold, gates of pearl, and walls of jasper. To me heaven will be a grand reunion. "And God shall wipe away all tears from their eyes, and there shall be no more death, neither sorrow, nor crying, neither shall there be any more pain, for the former things are passed away" (Revelation 21:4). That will be heaven to me.

It is my desire for this small book to help lift someone's heavy burden along the highway of life. My family members found our greatest help with the following:

1) Maintaining faith in God;
2) Shedding tears;
3) Sharing the grief with others, especially those who understand the death of a child;
4) Having the courage to go on with the normal activities of life, even when we didn't feel like doing so or thought we didn't have the strength to do so;
5) Trying to get adequate rest and exercise and continuing to eat a balanced, healthful diet.

As a general rule, even though other people are very well-meaning, it is not helpful to grieving parents to have religious beliefs imposed upon them with such statements as the following:

1) It was God's will;
2) God had a reason;
3) God has a purpose;
4) God had numbered his or her days, and it was your child's time;
5) God doesn't make mistakes;
6) God needed a rose for his garden;
7) God knows best;
8) God could be testing your faith;
9) Maybe God is trying to teach us something;
10) This was part of God's plan;
11) God takes the best.

Some very few people may be comforted by the above statements, but to most people they are hurtful, and they may be harmful to the point of causing some to become bitter and even to hate God.

What we have found more helpful is hearing people say

1) I am sorry;
2) I will remember you in my prayers;
3) I don't know what you're going through, but I feel for you;
4) I want you to know our thoughts are with you;
5) May God give you the strength you need to endure;
6) I know this to be almost more than you can bear.

It is also comforting to have people share their pleasant memories of the deceased.

In addition, we found the following behavior on the part of our friends clearly spoke their love and compassion:

1) Just being present with us, not necessarily saying anything;
2) Listening while we talked about the death and not trying to change the subject nor distract us;
3) Checking on us frequently for several months after Mary Lee's death;
4) Continuing to listen, even when they knew the stories as well as we did;
5) And, perhaps more than any other activity, writing us a letter—a letter that we read over and over many times.

ॐ

I want to close this section with two items, the first a story taken from Dr. Mendell Taylor's book, *Every Day With the Psalms*. Dr. Taylor was illustrating the perspective of viewing this moment's happenings against a concept of eternity. Here is his story:

> The nixie clerk in the post office is one who handles undeliverable mail, such as letters addressed to Santa Claus or Uncle Sam. One Christmas, a nixie clerk noticed that a letter addressed to Santa Claus was in the handwriting of his young daughter. He quickly opened the letter to see what was on her mind. He read:
>
> Dear Santa Claus: We are very sad at our house this year and I don't want you to bring me anything.

My little brother went to heaven last week and all I want you to do when you come to my house is to take his toys to him. I'll leave them in the corner by the chimney—his hobbyhorse and train and everything. You see, he'll be lost up in heaven without them, especially his horse. So you take them to him and you needn't leave me anything, but if you could give Daddy something that would make him stop crying, I do wish you would. I heard him say to Mummy that only eternity could cure him. Could you send some of that? And I will be your good little girl.—Marion.

And finally, a poem I've found most helpful:

The Serenity Prayer

God grant me the serenity
To accept the things I cannot change,
The courage to change the things I can,
And the wisdom to know the difference.

In Christian love and compassion,

Ted L. Wampler

IV

Four-and-a-half years after Mary Lee's death, a close friend of Mary Lee's family compiled a book for her children, Jim and Stephanie, as a Mother's Day gift. The book is composed of letters to the children written by friends and relatives of Mary Lee. In the letters, the writers recount stories about Mary Lee's life, their own "cherished memories" of her.

The book, while intended to provide the children with a lasting testimonial to their mother's life, has also helped all of us in Mary Lee's family—children, husband, sister, brothers, mother, and father—to remember, to laugh, and to heal.

I'm including here, with the permission of the authors, excerpts from those letters. All the letters are addressed to Jim and Stephanie.

❧ Susan White ☙

Cherished Memories of Mary Lee is a special memoir written by some of the dearest people to your mom. Their memories have been a blessing to them and are now a gift to you. . . . The purpose of this collection is to celebrate your mom's life and share with you some precious memories that you might not already know.

When I was sixteen I lost my dad. I would have loved to have known what he was like as a child, a teenager, and as a young adult. I had only known him as a parent. It was that desire that inspired this memoir.

These letters are full of stories about your mom and the special people in her life. Martha Fox shared with me one of her favorite "Mary Lee" stories. Almost every Saturday [she, another friend,] and your aunt Ruth Ann would go to the movies at the Tennessee Theater in Knoxville. . . . Occasionally Ruth Ann would bring along her little sister. The big girls didn't mind Mary Lee going with them [but] they didn't want to sit next to her, because whoever did had to hold her seat down through the whole movie. Mary Lee was so small the chair would always fold up on her unless someone else helped hold it down.

ဖာ Cindy Cook ဇ

In March of 1964, when I was eight years old, I moved to Lenoir City. [Mary Lee and I] immediately became inseparable. We spent more nights together than we did apart. My dad came to her house one day and asked if he could see me because I had been at her house so many days that he was beginning to wonder if I still existed.

I remember climbing Little Mountain, riding ponies, and eating jars of dill pickles with saltine crackers. We liked to dress exactly alike. By seventh grade . . . we also spent a lot of time at the nursing home visiting and singing to residents. Your mom was the kindest, most compassionate person I've ever known.

In the eighth grade, my desk was under a window, and one day the venetian blinds fell on me and cut my leg. I wouldn't go to the doctor for stitches without Mary Lee. I was so scared but she was so comforting. She told me to look on the bright side—maybe someone would drop an atomic bomb or maybe we would be raptured before we got to the doctor and I wouldn't have to have stitches at all.

No matter what I did, [Mary Lee] unconditionally loved me. In high school, when sometimes my focus wasn't the greatest, she was never judgmental, but she always knew how to reel me back in. She was such an example of God's love not just to me but to everyone, no matter whether it was at church or at school. I ask myself, what if I had never met her.

ॐ Joel Malone ॐ

Your mom . . . was a giver, not a taker. She loved people, and she did anything she could to help them. I was always astonished at the things she began at an early age, such as her visits to the nursing home. Most teens were too self-absorbed to ever consider ministering and caring for the aged, but [not] Mary Lee. Her stories about those she cared for were sweet, funny, and very caring. I think she often saw the humor in things to mask the sadness that she saw in so many of those folks. She loved and cared for them all. I am sure she was a real bright spot in their lives.

Mary Lee . . . had high standards for herself [and] lived to those standards. One time [I asked her] what she was going to do on her day off at the bank. She responded that she wanted to accomplish many tasks; most were related to her Christian beliefs. She told me that she got up early (like 6 a.m.) on her day off. I was amazed, because most of us at that age lived for sleeping late. Mary Lee told me that she had too much life to live to waste it sleeping.

ॐ Teddy Wampler ॐ

I had the privilege of being very close to Mary Lee [as] her little brother at Tennessee Tech. [She] helped me with everything [and] typed my important papers. She was better than a computer spell check program. She had fun doing it. She called me one night [during] my freshman year and said, "Teddy, spell women." I said, "W-E-M-O-N." After she stopped laughing, she explained it to me. I had written an entire biology paper about the reproductive system with men and wemon.

&ɔ JoAnn Neely England ᵓʒ

I'm not sure where to begin to tell you what a wonderful, nurturing person your mom was. First, I need to tell you that Mary Lee was a mentor to me during our college days. I could talk to Mary Lee about anything and she was like a mother: she always knew the right answers. I remember asking her questions like, "Why should I not do [something]. Who will know?" She always reminded me that I would know and God would know.

Mary Lee was our floor rep and . . . the most responsible young person that I knew. She [went] to bed at 10 p.m. and [arose] at 6 a.m., a habit almost unheard of in college.

[Because] 36 girls lived on our dorm floor and shared a telephone, . . . we had a five-minute phone limit for a local call and a 15-minute limit for long distance. Since I loved to talk and could hardly even say hello in five minutes, I always had a problem with this limit. Mary Lee would yell, "Phone limit" and I would always yell back, "It's long distance." She never fussed, but I know she knew the truth.

I'm not very good at writing, so I would always have Mary Lee proof my English papers. . . . Once I had written a paper about some furniture, which I referred to as chester drawers, and Mary Lee in her proofing had marked it out in red and put chest-of-drawers. I asked her if she was sure. I told her that in Tazewell [my hometown] we called it chester drawers.

She assured me that I was wrong and that it was just some type of slang we used in Tazewell.

[In later years Mary Lee] and I would talk for hours about our children, our hopes and dreams for them and just life in general. Mary Lee was proud of both of you and prayed for you both daily. She wanted you both to live life to its fullest, but she wanted you to always keep God first. . . . Your mom loved you very much, and she will live on forever in your hearts and in the hearts of others.

৵ Jody Cusick cয

I remember how your mother always treated everyone with great respect and never met a stranger. She could start a conversation with just about anyone. Once, when your parents were returning from a trip, they were delayed at the airport by bad weather. While standing in line, your mother started talking to some of the people around them. Several months later she got a birth announcement from one of the couples she had met. They wanted to share their joy with her and thank her for helping them at the airport.

৵ Melanie Amburn cয

[Your mother was] one of my dearest friends [and] was such a vital part of our lives [that] her absence has made an indescribable void in our hearts.

I have never known a more devoted and concerned mother than Mary Lee. The "log cabin" that was her home did not have central air conditioning, and [a few days after she brought him home from the hospital] Jimmy broke out in a heat rash [which] she fretted and worried over. Jimmy, she would show me your back and legs and neck, and I would tell her that it would be okay and that you were just gorgeous. She would just smile and say, "I know," and we would laugh and laugh. She always had a Jim story to tell. Once you asked for a ball in a local store and she replied to you that the store owner had no balls, [which] caused quite a stir with some of the older gentlemen customers.

ᛒᴐ Pam Breazeale ᴄᴈ

Mary Lee lived her life with a serious intent, but always with a funny story along the way. Her sense of humor was rivaled only by that of her sister Ruth Ann. An evening spent with the two was sure to leave you with an aching side from laughing so hard at whatever story they were telling.

Underneath all the humor your mother was constantly helping others by bringing their needs to the attention of those who could help. She cared deeply for others and made a difference in many lives. If someone needed money, food, help in finding a job, or maybe just someone to talk to, your mother always seemed to have time.

ᛒᴐ John Edd Wampler ᴄᴈ

My fondest memory of Mary Lee . . . comes from a cassette tape that Al gave to me the Christmas after Mary Lee's death. It is a tape of Mary Lee and a very young Jimmy and Stephanie singing "I Came to Love You Early" at Dixie Lee Baptist Church.

Prior to the song she reads the testimony of our Grandpa (Riley Marion Wampler) that he had buried in the cornerstone of an addition to the plant in the early 1960's. When it was dug up after his death[,] the vessel was . . . cracked open . . . and [the contents] read for the first time. Through his words,

[Mary Lee] refers to each member of our family (a family who knew that Mary Lee did in fact come to love the Lord early). Mary Lee never wavered from her faith.

&ɔ Larry Duff (Principal at Eaton Elementary) ȼȝ

Mary Lee took some graduate classes with teachers from Sevier County [and learned] how to do a walk-a-thon. She brought me the material to read and said if I approved she would be glad to be in charge of [the walk-a-thon]. I [hesitated]. [After several weeks] she stopped by the office and said, "If we are going to do that fund raiser we had better get started," so we did. We called it the Rainbow Romp. The first year it brought in around $20,000 and gradually increased . . . to [more than] $40,000 [annually].

&ɔ Cherie Williams ȼȝ

Mary Lee truly had a gift for storytelling. Someone else could tell a story, but it just wasn't the same as when Mary Lee told it. [Among the] many funny stories she told about things her students had said and done, my favorite was [about her first year of] teaching. [During a] unit on dinosaurs, she [had] the students name their favorite dinosaur, and she wrote the name on the board. One especially bright little boy named a dinosaur that she wasn't familiar with, so she wasn't sure how to spell the word. She always got a laugh from telling how he stood up in his seat and said, "Could we get a teacher in here who knows how to spell?"

Mary Lee had a real love for books and reading. She always laughed and said that Al didn't worry about her going shopping unless it was to a bookstore.

❦ Ruth Ann Denton ❧

Mary Lee always made quality time for both of you. One way she did this was by reading to you. She knew that children who are read to are given a real boost in learning. But I also know Mary Lee spent that time with you every night because she loved you with all her heart.

Our entire family will never be the same without Mary Lee in our lives. She brought so much to each of us with her zest for life. I could write a book about . . . memories from our childhood. After we became adults, she loved to get me in a crowd and embarrass me by making me tell all those evil things I used to do to her. Her favorite one was the time I stuck the ice cream cone on her nose. We always shared a room when we were growing up. She loved to make me tell about waking her up every night before I got in bed with her because I wanted to know if she was okay before I would get in bed. If I were thirsty I'd aggravate her until she would get up and get me a drink. Also, if I wanted her to check the door to make sure it was locked, I'd lie there and sing until she would get up and check. If she ever wanted to get me back, all she had to say was that she would grab me around the neck if I didn't hush. That would scare me to death. She loved that because then she was the victor.

We had many girl-to-girl talks [which] turned into woman-to-woman talks. I miss those very much. Mary Lee always encouraged me and gave me strength when I was down.

❦ Frances Wampler ❧

I will tell you about the time [Mary Lee] was trying to correct Teddy's English. I had taken the boys to town to shop, and Teddy had bought a toy. He wanted to show it to his father, who was in bed sick. Teddy told his dad that he buyed the toy, but Mary Lee said, "No, Teddy, I *bought* the toy." Teddy jumped down off the bed, put his fists on his hips, and said, "No, no, Mary Lee, *I* buyed it." That is one time among many that she tried to be a teacher to the rest of us.

She was always a good mother to the boys and a good sister to Ruth Ann. When the boys were punished, they would go to Mary Lee, take her by the hand, have her sit in a chair; then they would sit on her lap until they finished crying.

๛ Ted Wampler ๙

[Mary Lee] lived her life with meaning and purpose. That is the most rewarding and satisfying life a person can live. She had a way of making people from all walks of life feel comfortable in her presence. She was always ready to encourage her friends and extend a helping hand to those who had nothing to offer in return. Her love for God reflected in her relationships with her family, co-workers, students, neighbors, and strangers.

[She] was also a fun-loving person [who] never ran out of funny stories to tell. I am thankful now that the reflection of her life can be seen in the two of you. May the light of her life never go out as long as you live.

I believe if your mother could have left some parting word with you it would have been Proverbs 3: 5-6, "Trust in the Lord with all thine heart; and lean not unto thine own understanding. In all thy ways acknowledge him, and he shall direct thy paths."

It is much easier to write about the life of someone than it is to live a life worth writing about. Mary Lee lived a life worth writing about.

The Compassionate Friends Credo

We need not walk alone.
We are The Compassionate Friends.
We reach out to each other with love,
   with understanding and with hope.
Our children have died at all ages
   and from many different causes,
     but our love for our children unites us.
Your pain becomes my pain
   just as your hope becomes my hope.
We come together from all walks of life,
   from many different circumstances.
We are a unique family
   because we represent many races and creeds.
We are young, and we are old.
Some of us are far along in our grief,
   but others still feel a grief
   so fresh and so intensely painful
   that we feel helpless and see no hope.
Some of us have found our faith
   to be a source of strength;
   some of us are struggling to find answers.
Some of us are angry,
   filled with guilt or in deep depression;
   others radiate an inner peace.
But whatever pain we bring to this
   gathering of The Compassionate Friends,
   it is pain we will share

just as we share with each other
our love for our children.
We are all seeking and struggling
to build a future for ourselves,
but we are committed to building
that future together as we reach out
to each other in love
and share the pain as well as the joy,
share the anger as well as the peace,
share the faith as well as the doubts,
and help each other to grieve as well as to grow.
We need not walk alone.
We are The Compassionate Friends.

We invite all bereaved parents to attend the nearest chapter of The Compassionate Friends. As we think of other bereaved parents, we are reminded of an old church hymn, "Blest Be the Tie That Binds." The words of the third verse speak to us:

We share our mutual woes, our mutual burdens bear;
And often for each other flows the sympathizing tear.

The Fallen Walls

It was a dwelling place no more,
Of one we loved who lived within a while;
We knew her presence by her deeds;
We knew her nearness by her smile.

It was the instrument by which she worked;
They were her hands, her feet,
Muscle and bone and nerve she used,
To make her tale of years complete.

But dwellings crumble with the years;
Walls totter, timbers rot;
The tool from constant use wears out and fails;
This is our common lot.

We call it death, and dread the parting hour,
When the loved form at last is laid away.
We dread the tender rites that mark
The disposition of the common clay.

But lo! A greater truth we know;
Tho now the tenant dwells within no more;
She only moved away; she gained
Translation to a fairer shore.

Life ended to begin anew;
Beyond our sight she liveth still.
We can but dream of what she knows;
We can but trust our Father's will.

And trusting turn to common tasks,
Dreaming the while of life beyond the years.
God's perfect love holds her and us,
And God himself shall wipe away all tears.

Author unknown

There are many verses in the Bible that offer comfort.

The following are just a few taken from the Authorized King James Version.

Psalms 46:1   God is our refuge and strength, a very present help in trouble.

121:2   My help cometh from the LORD, which made heaven and earth.

147:3   He healeth the broken in heart, and bindeth up their wounds.

Grief is a burden we can share.
We need the support of other people.

Galatians 6:2   Bear ye one another's burdens, and so fulfil the law of Christ.

There is comfort and tears.

Mathew 5:4   Blessed are they that mourn: for they shall be comforted.

11:28   Come unto me, all ye that labour and are heavy laden, and I will give you rest.

God is not the cause of our tragedies,
God is our source of comfort.

II Corinthians 1:3-4   Blessed be God, even the Father of our Lord Jesus Christ, the Father of mercies, and the God of all comfort; Who comforteth us in all our tribulation, that we may be able to comfort them which are in any trouble, by the comfort wherewith we ourselves are comforted of God.

Hebrews 4:16   Let us therefore come boldly unto the throne of grace, that we may obtain mercy, and find grace to help in time of need.

God is with us in our darkest hours.

Hebrews 13:5   ... for he hath said, I will never leave thee, nor forsake thee.

Hope of seeing our loved ones again.

II Samuel 12: 23   But now he is dead, wherefore should I fast? can I bring him back again? I shall go to him, but he shall not return to me.

John 14: 2 -- 3   In my Father's house are many mansions: if it were not so, I would have told you. I go to prepare a place for you. And if I go and prepare a place for you, I will come again, and receive you unto myself; that where I am, there ye may be also.

Will Our Tears Forever Flow

In the words of King David "How long must I wrestle with my thoughts and every day have sorrow in my heart"? Psalms 13: 2 NIV

John answers while in exile on the island called Patmos. "And God shall wipe away all tears from their eyes; and there shall be no more death, neither sorrow, nor crying, neither shall there be any more pain: for the former things are passed away." Revelation 21: 4

Comments and Excerpts From Cards And Letters

I thank my wife, Frances for her love, understanding and support in helping me to have the courage to open my grieving heart while writing this book. It is my desire that this book will give people a better understanding of grief.

T. W.

I would like to say thank you to my husband, Ted, for the courage he had to put our grief in the book *Will Our Tears Forever Flow*. My wish is that readers of the book will better understand the grief of parents whose children have died, at any age, and from any cause. May it be a blessing, a help and comfort to all.

F. W.

Thank you for writing it -- -- -- it was bittersweet and I know it will help many people through an almost unbearable time. It is such a honest and positive book.

A. H.

There are no words to express the overflow of emotions we felt while reading your words of sorrow and faith. We will be donating this labor of love to our church library, so that others may learn, understand and grow in faith from all your book has to offer.

M. and N. M.

I would like to thank you for the book *Will Our Tears Forever Flow*. I found it beautifully written with all its painful truth about loss of love to the happy wonderful memories of a fine woman.

S. B.

Comments and Excerpts From Cards And Letters
(Continued)

I received a copy of your book *Will Our Tears Forever Flow*. I have really taken my time in reading it because every time I picked the book up and started reading it, I developed lumps in my throat and tears in my eyes and had to stop for a while. Your book is extremely well written and certainly reflects the wonderful, enduring faith of all of your family.

H. O.

I thought the book was excellent. I lost my oldest son three years ago. It has been the toughest thing that I have ever been through. Your book was helpful to me and I wanted to thank you.

G. S.

Even though I cannot possibly identify with the sense of loss that you and your whole family must feel, your expression of that sense made a huge impression on me. What a gift you have created for anyone who has the privilege of reading. It really makes one value each day and realize how at any moment a storm can enter our lives and change everything.

J. M.

Notice

Bulk purchases of this book for resale are available.

For information please contact:

Wampler Farm Sausage Company
781 Hwy. 70W
Lenoir City, TN 37771

or

Tennessee Valley Publishing
PO Box 52527
Knoxville, TN 37950-2527
email info@tvp1.com